Eyes of an Innocent
to
Eyes of a Terrorist

Translated from Arabic into English

Special thanks to the editorial team
and Linda Hopkins

Eyes of an Innocent
to
Eyes of a Terrorist

By Issam Diek

With Photographs
by the Author

ISBN 1-56715-046-2

First Printing, 2001

P.O. Box 265
Swansboro, NC 28584

Printed in the United States of America

Contents

The Mountains of Temptation.

The Holy Land

An Historical Preface

I WON'T RETURN. I shall perhaps never be able to return. Here in my new country I will set about my life, enjoying freedom of thought and behavior and continuing my quest for truth and affiliation.

I still do not know the name of my homeland. It has been called Israel, and Palestine; the Holy Land, and combat terrain; the Promised Land, and the land of Canaan. Its city is the City of Peace and murderers of prophets; its residents are innocents and blood butchers.

My homeland is a single, narrow piece of land of extraordinary beauty on which dozens of diverse ethnic groups have lived and continue to live. Over the course of history, as one people and their system of rule arrived, another left, and all have left remnants who made their home in the land and distinguished themselves from the others by their religion. In the Middle East, religion is more than creed: it is an individual's way of indicating his pedigree and his very identity.

The population of the Holy Land falls into three major categories: Jews, Christians, and Muslims, with various sects branching out within each group. There are the Ashkenazi Jews, the Sephardic Jews and the Samarians, the Eastern Christians and the Western Christians, the Muslims and the Druze.

Since ancient times, history and the Holy Bible have testified to the Jewish presence in the region. King David ruled the kingdom of the Jews one thousand years before Christ. He took Jerusalem as his capital, and his kingdom extended eastward to the plain of Kidron and to Ein Hayyoun to the west. David's son Solomon assumed rule following his father's death and added the regions of Judea and Israel to the kingdom. (The region of Judea today is part of the territory of the West Bank that has been turned over to Yasser Arafat.)

Israel split away from Judea after King Solomon's death in 721 B.C. The Assyrians overthrew the Kingdom of Israel, and then King Nebuchadnezzar of Babylonia (present-day Iraq) sacked the city of Jerusalem and drove its Jewish population into captivity in Babel. In 539 B.C. Cyrus, King of the Persians, destroyed Babylonia and permitted the Jews to return to the region of Judea, where they rebuilt Jerusalem and Solomon's Temple.

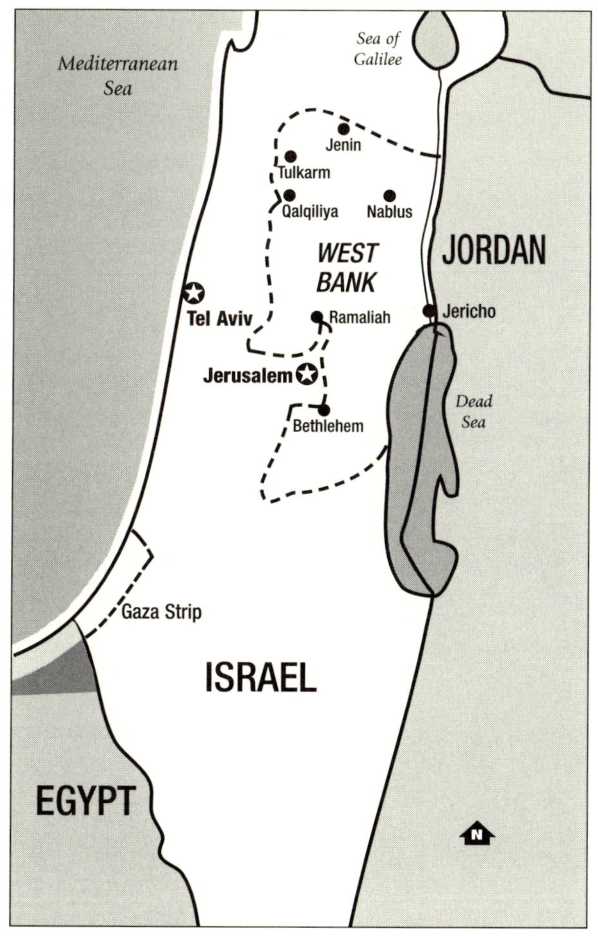

Mediterranean
Sea
Sea of
Galilee
Jenin
Tulkarm
Qalqiliya
Nablus
WEST
BANK
JORDAN
Tel Aviv
Ramaliah
Jericho
Jerusalem
Dead
Sea
Bethlehem
Gaza Strip
ISRAEL
EGYPT
N

The Dome of the Rock standing over the Temple Mountain in Jerusalem.

As the centuries passed, various foreign occupations of the area succeeded one another. Jews were dispersed into exile throughout all parts of the world.

Immediately following the establishment of the modern State of Israel in 1948, war broke out. The United Nations halted the war in the center of Jerusalem, dividing the city in two. West Jerusalem out to the Mediterranean Sea was recognized as the State of Israel, while East Jerusalem to the Jordan River was designated as the West Bank and placed under the rule of the King of Jordan. Rule of the Gaza Strip to the south, crammed in between the sea, Israel, and the Sinai, was assumed by Egypt. Once Israel was established, the state considered all its non-Jewish population to be Arabs and termed them Israeli Arabs.

In 1967 Israel found itself facing a new war with Egypt and Jordan. Israel won the war, and the borders of the state expanded to the Jordan River and the Sinai Desert, including the areas of the West Bank and the Gaza Strip. Israel imposed military rule on the populations of the two regions, which were primarily Christians and Muslims. The citizens of the West Bank were considered Jordanians, but those of the Gaza Strip were of undetermined nationality. The United Nations applied the name Palestinians to the residents of both areas as the most correct political term, following their British designation.

As a consequence of the theological and historical dispute between Muslims and Jews, Arabs launched a terrifying war against Israel and carried out their acts around the world. They created such politico-military organizations as the Palestinian Liberation Organization (PLO), under the leadership of Yasser Arafat, and the Islamic Jihad Movement. Arab nations supported them in the name of Arabism and Islam.

Arabs continued fighting with Israel, ignoring that all have a claim to the land and that they themselves were mainly settlers left behind by the Islamic occupations of the region and by Bedouins and commercial caravans from Hejaz (the west part of the Arabian Desert). They took up residence in the land to exploit its water and vegetation. In the middle of the seventh century, Arabs poured out from the heart of Hejaz and began their military-religious conquests. Their Caliph, Umar ibn al-Khattab, captured the city of Jerusalem and built the al-Aqsa and Dome of the Rock mosques on Solomon's Temple Mount, from which site Muslims believe the prophet Mohammed ascended into heaven.

Near the al-Aqsa Mosque, the Muslims built the mosque of Omar on a site where their Caliph had prayed. They built another Mosque of Omar directly facing the Church of the Nativity in the town of Bethlehem.

Muslim Arabs ruled the area for nearly four centuries; their settlements in the Holy Land increased, thus weakening the Jewish and Christian presence. In 1099 A.D. Pope Urban II declared war, rallying crusaders from various parts of Europe into the area, overthrowing the Muslims, and establishing a Christian state they called the Kingdom of Jerusalem.

A Palestinian child sits at the site of the Christ's manger in the Nativity Church. The Greek priest in charge of caring for the church stands nearby.

The Muslims recaptured the land from the crusaders in 1291 A.D., and established the age of the Mameluke sultans. Their rule lasted for two centuries, until the Ottoman Turks, also followers of Islam, took control. The Ottoman Empire continued for four centuries, ending with the British establishment of direct colonial authority over Palestine after World War I.

As a result of the repeated and lengthy Arab Islamic control of the area, its inhabitants—Jews, Christians, and Muslims—spoke Arabic as the official language of the state in addition to their native languages. During the age of the Turkish Sultans, adherence to Arabic was re-established due to Islamic dominance and the Arabization of society. When the State of Israel was created following the withdrawal of the British, the Jews of the Holy Land learned Hebrew, the language of their new nation. Non-Jews continued to speak Arabic, maintained an Arab society, and found their presence restricted to Arab areas. A certain Arab identity was thus imposed on the Christians of the Holy Land despite their having no ethnic, religious, or even social link with the Arabs.

Christians of the Holy Land are mainly the remnants of families of pilgrims, soldiers, or missionaries and their converts who settled the land during the period of the Christian empires in the Middle Ages. The Eastern Christians, most of whom are Greek Orthodox, are left over from the Byzantine presence, whereas most of the Armenians, Syrians, and Kurds migrated into the area as refugees.

During Palm Sunday religious services in Jerusalem, Palestinian Christians, Israeli Arabs, foreign pilgrims, and Arab clerics partici-pate in a march from the Mount of Olives through the streets of the Old City under strict guard by the Israeli police.

Palm Sunday religious services in Jerusalem.

Western Christians belonging to the Roman Catholic and Lutheran denominations, who represent a small part of the Christian minority in the Middle East, are mainly the descendants of European families who traveled to the Holy Land during the time of the Crusades. Following the Muslim recapture of the Holy Land, and due to the crimes committed by Crusader soldiers against Muslims and Jews when they entered Jerusalem, the western churches hid all documents indicating the origins of the families in their denominations to protect them from Muslim revenge. Most of them changed their last names and took on Arabic names that were little more than descriptions.

Even today in the Holy Land, on the eve of the twenty-first century, religion defines where an individual or family will live, how they will live, with whom they will live, and what language they will speak. Not nationality, nor social or political affiliation, but religion!

I myself was born in Bethlehem in 1969 into a Western Christian family. Bethlehem is one of the towns of the West Bank and the area of Judea. I was born there while it was under the rule of the State of Israel. My brother, who is three years older than I, was also born there, but at that time it was ruled by the Kingdom of Jordan. Likewise, my father was born there, but at a time when it was one of the towns of Palestine under British rule. I emigrated from my town in 1993 while it was still being governed by Israel. However, just a few years later Israel surrendered Bethlehem and its populace to Yasser Arafat's authority.

Neither I, my brothers and sister, my parents, nor my grandparents have ever seen peace or lived freely in Bethlehem, the City of Bread and the birthplace of the Christ. Outbreaks of war and disputes have been constant throughout history due to the presence of so many peoples with differing political, religious, and social convictions. Always, one party was in power, while other parties were leading violent resistance or being victims. There has always been ruler, killer, and victim.

Little girl from Bethlehem.

In the Nativity Church.

Beit Lei'hem

BETHLEHEM IS A PRETTY, QUIET CITY situated on a hill covered with fig and olive trees. The Church of the Nativity stands proudly in the town center. Its residential quarters are filled with both ancient stone alleyways and modern streets lined with commercial shops and recreational centers. Its residents are Christians and Muslims; Jews live in settlements outside the town.

Originally, the Christians of Bethlehem comprised 80 percent of the population. After the 1948 war, their percentage gradually shrank to less than 25 percent as Muslim villagers and refugees moved into the city to take advantage of its good living conditions and the hospitality of its residents. Muslim families received financial subsidies from international Islamic

The Nativity Church on Christmas evening.

agencies, encouraging them to remain in the land and purchase Christian properties. By offering double the price, they ensured that sale to them would be approved. Meanwhile, many of the young men and women of Christian families emigrated to escape the burgeoning social and political pressures in the area. They scattered all over the earth, making new homes in foreign lands to secure a better future for themselves and their children.

The increase in Muslim population and the strengthening of their presence in the city led to an immediate threat to Christian lifestyle and freedom of choice. The Muslims despised Christians and their way of life, and they sought to take over governance of the city and impose the laws of Islam. Islam's holy book, the Koran, calls Christians and Jews polytheists and accuses their societies of being decadent. Any social or political behavior that does not adhere to Islamic law is deemed a corruption, against which the believing Muslim must fight to set right. The Koran bans Muslims from giving allegiance to a Christian or Jew: "O ye who believe! Take not the Jews and the Christians for your patrons and protectors; they are but patrons and protectors to each other. And he amongst you that turns to them [for allegiance] is of them. Verily Allah guideth not a people unjust" (Koran, Chapter of the Table, verse 51). The Chapter of Family of Imran, verse 28, confirms this: "Let not the believers take for allegiance unbelievers rather than believers: if any do that they shall have no relation left with Allah except by way of precaution, that ye may guard yourselves from them. But Allah cautions you to fear Himself for the final goal is Allah."

Inasmuch as Muslims believe that the Koran is the sublime word of God revealed from heaven, a Muslim believes he must strive to accomplish the demands of Allah as recorded in that sacred work: "And fight the Polytheists altogether" (Chapter of the Repentance, verse 36), for "Mohammed is the Messenger of Allah and those who are with him are strong against unbelievers" (Chapter of the Conquest, verse 29).

Our perspectives as Christians, our customs and traditions, our way of life and thinking, all are deemed an abomination to the Muslim world. Beginning in late 1988 when Israel started to lose the ability to impose security in all areas, and after Israel gave up Bethlehem and its citizenry to Yasser Arafat's authority in 1994, PLO and Islamic movements took over that arena, forced the public to submit to their orders, and imposed control through threats and terror. The residential population's liberty vanished. With no one to defend them, their civil rights were openly and brazenly violated. If any tried to complain, they faced severe consequences.

Muslim oppression of non-Muslims in the Holy Land, the Middle East, and worldwide is not only due to historical and political disagreements, combined in some instances with alternating land claims, but also because of the teachings of Islam itself.

*An art exhibition presented by young Israeli Arab women in Jerusalem.
Such exhibits encountered the opposition of extremist Muslims who
considered them decadence and dissolution that must be
fought by believing Muslims.*

Christian Palestinian, who lives near Bethlehem, suffered a loss when his herd of pigs was poisoned by Islamic fundamentalists.

According to Islamic views, the people of the earth are divided into two groups: Muslims, who have surrendered themselves to God, believe in His Koran, and are committed to His Prophet Mohammed; and non-Muslims, pagans and polytheists who are the enemies of Islam and against whom a Muslim must wage war. No matter what else a man may be in this world, he is either a Muslim, who will fight for God's cause when jihad is declared, or a non-Muslim, whom sooner or later the danger of Islam will reach. Muslims will fight any non-Muslim and his country in order to raise their banner. The only peaceful way open to polytheists to stop the fighting—as stated in the Koran—is submission to the rule of Islam and payment of the jizya, the head tax on non-Muslims. As for pagans, only the embracing of Islam is acceptable from them.

The Koran has provided instructions to Muslims: "Fight those who believe not in Allah nor the Last Day, nor hold that forbidden which hath been forbidden by Allah and His Messenger, nor acknowledge the religion of truth, from among the People of the Book, until they pay the jizya with willing submission, and feel themselves subdued" (Chapter of Repentance, verse 29). In the Chapter of the Women, verse 76, the Koran adds: "Those who believe fight in the cause of Allah, and those who reject faith fight in the cause of evil. So fight ye against the friends of Satan. Feeble indeed is the cunning of Satan."

In the Chapter of Repentance, verse 5, the Koran confirms: "Then fight and slay the Polytheists wherever ye find them, and seize them, beleaguer them, and lie in wait for them every stratagem [of war]; but if they repent and establish regular prayers, and pay Zakat [tithes] then open the way for them. For Allah is Oft-forgiving, Most Merciful."

During the last few decades, Muslim activity has concentrated on restoring nonreligious Muslims to religious practice and constructing a strong grassroots base as a springboard for the Islamic revolution as it works against governments and societies that do not adhere to the teachings of Islam. They call this activity the silent jihad, because jihad is battle, and the preparation for battle is silent jihad. Islamic leaders are convinced that this believing Islamic grassroots base is the primary force that will enable the successful establishment of the Islamic Nation and deliver rule to the caliph, or Amier of Islam. Many of these leaders believe this caliph will lead Islamic conquests East and West launched from Palestine, the heart of the world.

To that end, under the concept of the silent jihad, Islamic organizations and movements have worked to build their religious grassroots bases in all parts of the world. Consequently, the silent jihad has confirmed its success. Islam has become one of the most rapidly growing and widely spread religions in the world. Societies in the Islamic countries of the Middle East and the Far East have clearly been affected by religious extremism. In Britain alone nearly 900 churches have been converted to mosques. More than four million Muslims live in the United States of America, where they have built missionary centers

Muslim students in the University of Bethlehem.
The university was established and is funded by the Vatican.

*Palestinian Muslims demonstrate against Israel in front
of the Israeli consulate general in San Francisco, California.*

and created narrow-minded concentrations of people in all U.S. cities, many of its small towns, and in the countryside.

Organizations such as the Islamic Jihad movement, the Islamic Liberation Movement (Hamas), the Muslim Brotherhood, Hezbollah, al-Qa'ida movement, the Groups of Caution and Transmission, the Islamic Resistance Front, and others depend on people's social and economic problems for their missionary activity. In addition, methods of terrorism, arousal of zeal, and stories of scientific miracles in the Koran have enabled Islam to attract man's mind.

Once the faltering Muslim or the newly believing member of Islam has been strengthened, Islamic organizations offer him the opportunity to impose the jihad in the cause of God. At that point it becomes very difficult for a believing Muslim to refuse jihad. How could he refuse, since jihad is a religious obligation and the Koran has prepared and presented him to the faith through jihad, such is his faith in God. The Koran, the word of God literally revealed from heaven, not only states that God's religion is Islam and that anyone desiring any religion other than Islam will not be accepted, but also demands that the faithful follower battle for the cause of God. The Chapter of the Cow, verse 244, states: "Then fight in the cause of Allah, and know that Allah heareth and knoweth all things."

The Koran refers to the need for a Muslim to commit to God's teachings and admonitions, regardless of their nature, because that is the best path to follow. The Chapter of the Women, verse 66, states: "If we had ordered them to sacrifice their lives or to leave their homes, very few of them would have done it. But if they had done what they were [actually] told, it would have been best for them, and would have gone farthest to strengthen their [faith]."

The Koran arouses zeal to get Muslims out for battle. This arousal of zeal, the epitome of conviction, is a successful means used to purchase a Muslim's life and happiness in this world in exchange for promises of his reward in the afterlife: "Let those fight in the cause of Allah who sell the life of this world for the hereafter. To him who fighteth in the cause of Allah, whether he is slain or gets victory, soon shall we give him a reward of great value" (Chapter of the Women, verse 74). In the Chapter of Repentance, verse 111, the Koran confirms: "Allah hath purchased of the Believers their persons and their goods; for theirs [in return] is the Garden [of Paradise]. They fight in His Cause, and slay and are slain."

In his quest for martyrdom and entrance to paradise, a Muslim fears neither death nor harm. Whatever happens to him, according to his religious teachings, will be God's written destiny for him. That destiny will be his even were he to remain hidden in his house. According to the Chapter of the Women, verse 78: "Wherever ye are, death will find you out, even if ye are in towers built up strong and high! If some good befalls them they say, 'This is from Allah.' But if evil, they say, 'This is from thee,' [O Prophet]. Say: 'All things are from Allah.' But what hath come to these people that they fail to understand a single fact?"

Boys learning the Koran in mosques in Jerusalem.

Girls learning the Koran in Jerusalem.

Just as Islam demands jihad of Muslims, it also demands that they incite jihad. Verse 65 of the Chapter of the Spoils of War affirms: "O Prophet! Rouse the Believers to the fight. If there are twenty amongst you, patient and persevering, they will vanquish two hundred. If a hundred, they will vanquish a thousand of the Unbelievers, for these are a people without understanding."

Frequently over the years I have attended Muslim services in their mosques. I have even performed their prayers with them in my search for facts. The nature of the sermons and invocations that the imams preached to the worshippers aroused my interest. One of these invocations was one that I heard so frequently that it is embossed in my memory, just as it is in the memory of the worshippers.

Once the prayer has concluded, turning right and then left, the worshippers chant after the imam: "Peace be upon you and the mercy of God. Peace be upon you and the mercy of God." In accordance with this teaching of revelation, they bid farewell to man, demons, angels, and all who participated with them in performing prayers. The imam then raises his hands and chants his invocation. The worshippers respond to him in faith:

"O God, accept our prayers from us and open the gates of Heaven to our pleas."

"Amen."

"O God, bring the Muslims together, and have mercy of their dispersion."

"Amen."

"O God, cut off the progeny of the pagans and polytheists."

"Amen."

"O God, do away with the Jews and burn their crops."

"Amen."

"O God, establish the nation of Islam and the Muslims."

"Amen."

"O God, strengthen Islam and give us victory over the pagans and the polytheists."

The imam adds and worshippers reply, "Amen."

*Palestinian Muslims praying on the Temple Mountain square,
outside al-Aqsa mosque in Jerusalem.*

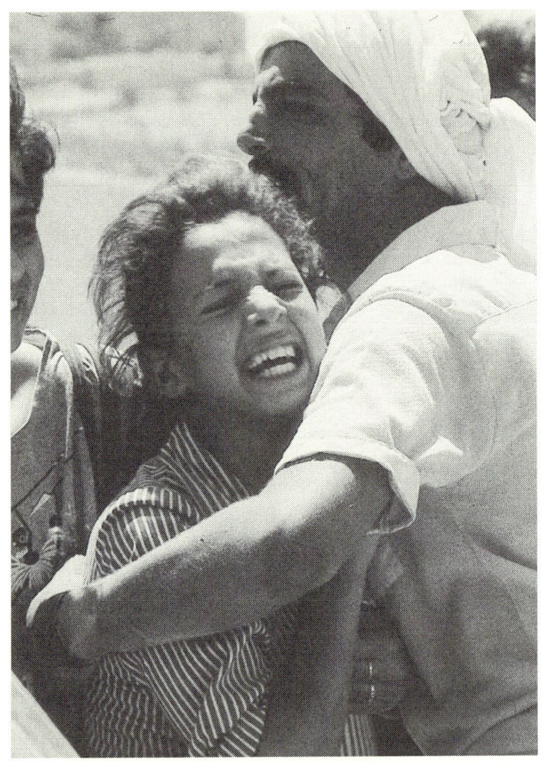

A Palestinian girl just after hearing of the murder of her younger brother during fighting that broke out between Palestinians and Israeli military forces in the village of al-Ta'amira, near Bethlehem.

Victims

In the Middle East, in the middle of the conflict and acts of terrorism, we—Christians, Jews, and Muslims alike—stood silently around the scenes of killing and bloodshed, our eyes open as wide as they could be lest the specter of death catch us off guard, but wanting to close them so we would no longer have to view the horrifying colors of terrorism. We were sick of the blood, the black of fires, and the eyes of the victims. We only wanted peace and an end to the bloodshed. Nothing in all of creation was worth the crimes that sick minds were perpetrating.

The continual Arab and Islamic fight against the Israeli presence in the Holy Land has intensified in the past twelve years, transforming the cities and villages in the areas of conflict into graveyards of the living. Aspects of civilization and order disappeared. Barricades, barrels, and discarded wheels are scattered throughout the streets and alleys. Residents rush

Palestinian Demonstration.

to do their shopping before clashes outbreak or strikes are imposed, whereupon life would cease in public places. The walls and doorways of buildings are awash with graffiti painted in discordant colors. A dreadful silence fills the streets. Citizens, soldiers, and visitors all look on warily, fearfully, as the winds of terrorism storm, turning streets and neighborhoods into an inferno and filling the quiet with the screams.

Not even the foreign tourist could escape the hand of terrorism. During the summer of 1989, two young German tourist women were stabbed in the middle of the day in the crowds of East Jerusalem. Their blood spilled out on the ancient ground in front of Damascus Gate, one of the entrances to the old city. They were killed not very far from the Church of the Ascension, the Wailing Wall, and the al-Aqsa Mosque. A young Palestinian shouted, "Allah is Great!" in Arabic before making the first knife thrust. When the second woman tried to rescue her companion, he stabbed her too, and then ran off toward the marketplace in the Old City.

At the time I was working as a reporter and photographer for the daily newspaper *al-Fajr*. I was part of a media team covering the northern section of the West Bank when we received the news of the stabbing. It came as no surprise, for the plaza at Damascus Gate is often the scene of stabbing incidents, especially targeted towards Orthodox Jews as they head from West Jerusalem to the Wailing Wall or to their quarter in the Old City.

We returned to Jerusalem. At the newspaper office, I saw a picture of the incident on the editor's desk: a knife smeared with blood lying on a table under the watchful eye of a police-man. The corner of the table in the picture blocked out the face of a girl lying on her back under the feet of security officers and medical personnel. Her blouse had been torn apart, revealing her upper body. She was wearing light summer slacks, and her feet were bare. She had been a beautiful young woman.

Just before Christmas in 1989, another tourist, a sixty-year-old French woman, and her husband were sitting down to have lunch with their friends in a tourist restaurant in the town of Bethlehem. The man waiting on their table was a young Muslim Palestinian, who, for no reason and without any warning, wielded a knife in his hand, shouted, "Allah is great!" and lunged at the woman, stabbing and killing her. He killed her in front of her husband and friends, just a few steps away from the Church of Christ's Nativity.

The killer was a resident of the village of al-Ta'amera in the Bethlehem district. A member of his family stated to the news that his relative carried out this act because of the pressure of everyday life he felt in the village, in addition to his recent leaning toward the radical Islamic side.

It was a sad fact that the relative was stating. Young people often live under very difficult economic and survival pressure, with the result that they turn toward political and religious extremism to divert their despair through acts of terrorism and the murder of innocents rather than looking for the real cause of the pressure and solving the root of the problem. That French lady had come to Bethlehem as a tourist, as a visitor to the Church of the Nativity, a sacred religious site, offering her respect and reverence and delighting in her faith. She and her husband, and other tourists like them, are not only visitors, but are also a primary source of the city's economy and the income of the people who work there. That lady was part of her killer's livelihood. She was not to blame for his suffering, or that of the Palestinian people.

Years have passed and the conflict continues to find no end. The clashes grow more severe, and the number of Palestinian dead and injured mount. They include a significant number of children, which arouses the anger of the international public and human rights organizations. Those organizations accuse Israel of criminal behavior but remain silent about the fact that the Palestinian leadership violate the rights of their own children and endanger their lives by sending them into the ranks of demonstrators to take part in fighting on the lines of confrontation.

In addition, the PLO and radical Muslim leadership choose the public markets, the residential quarters, the schools, and places of worship as sites for instigating violent action against the military forces, using civilian concentrations, including children and the elderly, to provide them with human shields. This is why so many innocents fall to the bullets, the gas canisters, and the stones.

For my part, I have witnessed many scenes of citizens in the public markets running in every direction, racing for their

Rushing away from the market place in Gaza City.

lives, and silently praying to God after a group of masked men touched off an engagement with the military patrols. Women carrying goods suddenly abandoning them; vegetables and fruit scattering between helpless, tangled, kicking feet; elderly people with failing strength unable to flee, clutching their canes as they sought somewhere to hide; young women screaming out for a child or a mother; young men desperate to get out of the area before being rounded up and charged with complicity. Absolute pandemonium reigned.

As a reporter, I crouched behind walls to protect myself, lifting my cameras, shooting pictures, and loathing what I was seeing. Palestinian "strugglers" making war against a regular army, and using innocent human beings for their protection. They would then turn tail and run away before those people could hide! I took my pictures and prayed that I would not have to hear a scream of pain from the mouth of a child or some old person, some youth or soldier, or from my own mouth.

With the falling of new victims, a larger demonstrations would soon break out and more victims would fall. Young men and young women, boys, girls, mothers, and elders all went out to wage war against Israel. Each person had a dear one, a relative or a brother in Islam, killed or wounded while sacrificing himself or herself on their behalf.

Moreover, Palestinian demonstrators succeeded, in many ways, in embroiling Christians in their fight against Israel. On Sundays and holidays, demonstrators lay in wait for Christians to come out of their churches to ignite clashes with the Israeli security forces. One Christian would get injured or killed, and others would explode angrily against Israel and join the ranks of the Palestinian fighters.

Palestinian Demonstration in Bethlehem.

Palestinian demonstration in the city of West Bank, Ramallah.

Lucy

As a journalist, when incidents progressed and the number of fatalities grew, I lost interest in following the names of the daily casualties. One day I received news of several injuries in Bethlehem as a result of clashes that had broken out that morning. As usual, I paid it no significant attention, finished my workday, and that evening went home. My mother was waiting for me.

"Surely you've heard what happened in town today," she said, starting our conversation.

"Demonstrations at al-Madbasa street, with three injured," I answered, disinterested.

"And do you know who was injured?"

I turned toward her, suddenly full of anxiety. There must be some important news I hadn't heard. I wanted not to ask, so I wouldn't know. Answering before I could speak, my mother said, "Lucy."

"Lucy!" I answered, surprised.

Lucy was a very close friend of mine. A Christian social worker, she sometimes fed me leads on stories. She was strong, a fighter who really cared about people's civil rights and wanted to make a difference. She had always dreamed of peace.

"Impossible!" I protested. "Lucy had nothing to do with this fight; she can't stand it."

"You know, my son, it is always the innocent who suffer."

"How is she?"

"A bullet hit her in the hip. It is not dangerous, but it's not minor either. She's at the al-Hussein Hospital now."

"How did you learn about it?"

"Your aunt told your grandma, and your grandma called me."

I wasn't sure I could depend on news that had reached my mother from my aunt via my grandmother, so I raced to the hospital. Unfortunately Lucy was there. It saddened me to see her lying on the bed in pain following the surgical operation to have the bullet removed. Her condition did not allow her to talk very long, but she told me what had happened. She was on her way to work when young men with their faces covered suddenly appeared and began hurling stones at an Israeli patrol. She found herself surrounded in the middle of the clash with no place for protection. The soldiers fired at the stone throwers, and she was hit.

Several weeks passed before Lucy regained her health. Her favorite hobby became taking trips out of Bethlehem to go to Jerusalem, either to the Christian quarter or West Jerusalem as a respite from home and the tumult of the conflict. Many young men and women from the West Bank seek to visit the Jewish markets in Jerusalem for recreation and to reduce the pressure, despite threats from the Palestinian leadership against them.

"I was worried about you," I told Lucy once when we were together.

"I was afraid. I didn't know what was going to happen to me. I was trapped between the stones on one side, and the bullets on the other." She paused for a moment, then added, "It could have ended a lot worse than with a bullet in the hip."

"A bullet in the hip is bad enough!"

"The bullet made me a hero in everyone's eyes, a struggler, without having to do anything," she said dismissively.

"Let's thank the bullet for not making you a martyr!"

"A martyr on behalf of homeland and freedom? That would be interesting," she laughed playfully.

Israeli Border Policeman standing guard in the Muslims quarter of the Old City of Jerusalem.

"As far as I'm concerned, I'd rather be an ordinary citizen and alive than a dead hero."

"You say that, but you're the one who places himself in danger every day for a photograph or a story!"

I didn't answer. What was the use of answering; she knew that was my job. Continuing, she asked, "Have you ever found yourself embroiled in a situation like the one I was in, in the middle of a clash where you could do nothing to save your own life?"

"Few times," I replied. "I have had to stand helpless between demonstrators and the army, not daring to go in the direction of either side. The demonstrators would accuse me of acting in Israel's favor, which could cost me my life, and the army, as usual, would detain me on the charges of covering the news in a closed military area; that is, if they didn't accuse me of incitement simply for being a journalist who lives in the West Bank."

"And what do you do?"

"If I can't find a way out of the situation by avoiding both sides, I go over to the army. They at least know what they're doing."

"Have you ever been hit?" she asked.

"Stones, rocks, rubber bullets, and gas; but I was luckier than you." I thought back and added, "None of that terrified me as much as when a colleague of mine nearly had to kill a child before my very eyes to save his life and mine."

It happened in 1990 as I was taking a newspaper tour near the Hebron district with the Agence France Press correspondent, Patrick Baz. We went into the village of Yatta and found a large number of its young men and women gathered in the village center preparing for a demonstration or march. Patrick stopped the car, and we headed on foot toward the young men to let them know who we were and why we were there. It was not difficult to identify the leader of the group. He was a hot-headed young man who approached us surrounded by others, and asked the familiar questions.

The interrogation process took but a few minutes. We were asked questions which we had to answer: "Who are you? Who are you working for? Do you have any proof of identity with you? Does anyone in the village know you? Who sent you? Why did you come here today?" Our hot-headed friend then had to make his decision. Either we were desirable journalists because we worked for the Palestinian side or an acceptable foreign news agency, or we were undesirable journalists because we work for an agency they reject, or we are not journalists but rather Israeli intelligence. That friend is the one who knows who we are, not us or our official identity papers!

The interrogation ended, and then it was time to act on the decision. Those are the moments that always make me tense. We either get permission to stay, are welcomed as guests, and enjoy getting full news coverage plus a glass of tea or chilled juice, or we are chased out in a hail of stones and curses. Even worse, we may be beaten up and have our lives threatened.

Patrick and I weren't lucky this time. The response was negative, very negative. We ran to the car, and Patrick started the engine. In the meantime, the village residents had begun to crowd around us yelling and throwing stones. Patrick drove a few meters then stopped. Crouched down in my seat, I asked him what the problem was. He signaled me to look in front of the car. There was a three or four-year-old child standing in front of the car holding a stone in his hand. There was no way we could avoid him on the narrow village street. The screaming throngs were approaching, and the stone throwing was intensifying. Larger rocks were being hurled too. The car was outfitted with stone resistant windows, but they could not withstand that many stones that close. The windows began to break down, and we found that both of our lives were in danger. Patrick was overcome with anxiety, and I stayed helplessly silent. Throngs of "strugglers" were now alongside and on top of the car. Not one of them had the courage to stand in front of it except for this child. We knew that the windows could not take the abuse much longer. Patrick's eyes were transfixed on the child, his hands holding the steering wheel and his foot steady on the gas pedal. If he took off he would kill the child; if he waited, we would both be killed. Finally, the child made the move that saved his life and ours. He threw the stone at the car and took off running. He acted just like the demonstrators he had probably seen in his residential quarter and on television. He threw his stone and fled, thankfully opening the road ahead of us, very thankfully indeed.

Front yards and public squares become schools for the
Palestinian children to learn from.

Neither Patrick nor I had threatened the life of that child. Any thought we may have had of harming him was that of a quarry under threat and having no option. The lives of all three of us were being threatened. Preoccupied with stoning, beating, and killing us, not one of the villagers cared enough for the safety of the child to get him out of the way. Had something dreadful happened to him, we would have been counted among the criminal dead; the villagers would have been the peaceful innocents. I thanked God a thousand times that I was not the driver that day.

Palestinian mother swears by the name of 'Allah' against Israel in Gaza Strip.

Mentality

~

THE NATURE OF MY WORK and that of my colleagues in Israel, and the fact that we moved frequently between the two contending sides, always endangered our safety. The primary threat was usually misjudgment or a bad decision made and announced by the leader of a party or demonstration. Those leaders made themselves judges, with no attorneys for the defense, and without evidence to support their accusation; a people's kangaroo court lacking in wisdom. Once the verdict is declared the crowd rushes to execute it. It was sad for me to watch how a word, just one word, could sway a group of people right or left. If someone accused you of being a traitor, you were finished. If someone else called you a struggler, you'd be a king! This was one reason innocents were being killed at the hands of Palestinians, and all the while it also helped Israel plant its agents among Palestinian ranks and guaranteed their safety.

During one of my tours covering the news I was accompanied by Essais Baitel, the chief photographer from France's Gamma agency at that time. We had gotten word from a local agent of the likelihood of a people's march being held in the village of Abu Fallah, south of the Nablus district, to celebrate the anniversary of the founding of the Fatah movement, which is one of the members of the Palestinian Liberation Organization, headed by Yasser Arafat.

We entered the village, walked away from the car, introduced ourselves, and were received. A tremendous number of young men, women, and elderly people crowded around us as if we had come from outer space. They asked us all the usual questions and told us various bits of news. One of them, a man with a long beard, shouted out for no reason at all, "They are intelligence!" Then he repeated himself, swearing this time, "By God, intelligence!" Everyone turned toward him, as did we. Essais doesn't speak Arabic, but he knew the word for "intelligence" very well and what the consequences of that reference to us would be. Everyone fell silent, while our sheikh continued to yell. Others began joining in the chant for no reason. The villagers accepted the accusation, crowded in on us, and began screaming in our faces. The situation terrified us because the screaming would soon turn to angry slaps and blows with no way out.

Essais looked at me, clearly nervous. It was, of course, my turn to act. I was the one who spoke Arabic, so I was supposed to know how to deal with these people. Talking was useless;

the trial had ended before being held. There was no one left in the chamber to listen. I could find no way to defend ourselves or get out of the situation. I gave up quietly, apologizing to Essais, to myself, and to my mother who would have news of us before the evening was over. I stood waiting for heaven's mercy, or even that of the devil. I hated being defeated weakly and silently. I began screaming at them without thinking, mercilessly slaying my fear: "Idiots! Fools! If we really were intelligence we would have pulled our weapons before you got so close! Go ahead, hit us! Kill us! Innocent victims to be added to your list of ignorance! If we really were who you claim, where are the military forces racing to rescue us the moment we were detected!"

A miracle happened. They fell silent. They exchanged glances and began to draw back. My screaming had gotten through to them. My words had penetrated their minds. I had learned a new technique. They believed in our innocence. Their irate fury eased, and then quieted. Heads bowed, and mouths muttered. We weren't going to wait around for the march, lest it become a funeral. Our feet moved quickly back to the car, and we left the village cursing the hour we had entered. Essais went on telling our colleagues, "He saved my life." I hadn't; I had actually given up.

From that day on Essais became my permanent companion on the coverage team. He was one of the finest international photojournalists in the profession. We worked together for over three years while we covered all phases of the Israeli-

Palestinian conflict. We watched it begin and followed the events as they progressed. We beat out all the other teams, and our names became known in all areas. The key for our success laid in the fact that when we found a need to cover a story or report, we would cover it regardless of whether it was possible, difficult, or impossible.

We covered stone throwing, setting of fires, screams, firing of bullets, beatings, demolition, acts of terrorism and crime, popular armies and their marches, masked men and the injured, the dead and their funerals, and we even got access to armed Palestinian cells in their hideouts. We spoke to them and took their pictures. As the conflict dragged on, daily incidents became the norm and Israeli-Palestinian talks grew boring, so we reduced our news coverage and concentrated on doing a documentary about the sources of the conflict and its impact on the various people involved. We covered the stories of people and lived their daily lives with them, from politicians to farmers and fishermen, students of Islamic law to Christian nuns in their convents. That is when we began to uncover facts as if we were opening graves in which jewels had been buried.

Essais frequently spoke to me about the wars he had covered around the world. They included the Lebanese war, and I wished I had been there with him to photograph the people before they became remnants of war. He, too, wished that he had been with me in 1989 when I met the Palestinian death squad known as Black Panther.

Palestinian women reaping wheat from the Mount of Temptation.

Gaza Beach

The Black Panther cell consisted of a group of armed young men who were members of the Fatah movement. They had taken the old city in the town of Nablus as their headquarters because its labyrinth of narrow alleyways made it difficult for the Israeli army to reach them there. In people's eyes their mission was to execute Palestinian collaborators and spies working for Israel, but in reality the cell was used simply to terrorize and kill the movement's enemies, including Israel's collaborators. The Fatah command would provide the cell with a list of names, and its members would then assume the task of executing them. In addition, the Popular Front of the PLO set up an armed cell parallel to Black Panther, which it named Red Eagle. It also assumed the mission of executing Israel's collaborators and the Front's enemies.

Both cells steadfastly refrained from getting involved in armed clashes with Israeli security forces, regardless of the reason, to avoid Israel becoming even angrier with them and intensifying its pursuit. For the PLO, the activities of these armed groups within the Palestinian arena were of greater importance than their actions against Israeli forces.

At that time, Majda el-Batsh, an editor of the *al-Fajr* newspaper's weekly magazine *al-Usbuu` al-Jadeed*, had contacted me. She asked me to accompany her on a business trip to the town of Nablus for a two-day visit.

"Nablus?" I asked.

"Yes. You'll enjoy the trip. Trust me."

I did trust her. The next morning we boarded a taxi to the town, where we met the people Majda wanted to interview while I took their pictures. When the evening's work was over we went to the home of a Nablus family who hosted us for that night.

After sharing dinner with the family—consisting of the father, mother, and a baby girl—Majda went off to sleep, and I sat with the father high up on the apartment's fourth floor balcony, with a mesmerizing view of the town laid out before us. As we turned to discussing the Black Panther group, he explained the technical aspects of their activities.

"Once the cell receives a list of names, the group's members and their accomplices lie in wait in the markets and public places for those wanted and then 'drag' them off into the old city, where they are executed. When someone is 'dragged' off the street, we know that a corpse will be dumped somewhere."

"However, if they lay in wait for very long and the wanted persons do not show up, the group waits until dark and the early morning hours to surround their residence. They will be dragged off from there. Black Panthers enjoy the power to act and move inside the town because of their many hideouts. Based on the information provided to them by their accomplices, they are able to get to anyone they want."

"We heard about a woman who was hanged yesterday, and whose body was found suspended in the middle of the marketplace this morning. Was she a collaborator?" I inquired.

"Only God, Fatah, and the victim know." He responded crisply, then sighed as he contemplated the soft lights of the old city.

"I want to go into that town," I told him.

"Why? To photograph the executions and the hanging corpses?"

"I want to talk to the people and photograph what I see."

"The only journalists allowed to enter the old city are local citizens who are well known to PLO affiliates, or more accurately, its members."

"That's going to change, because I'm going in too."

"You're not serious, are you?"

"Yes, I'm serious. Majda will take the taxi back to Jerusalem around noon, and I'm heading into the old city."

"Impossible. Are you out of your senses?"

"My senses I leave at home, so they won't get in the way of my work."

"You're a stranger for them! If you go in there carrying your cameras, you'll never get out safely. That's if you get out at all."

"That's why I'm going to take a local journalist from our agent's office, here in town, along with me."

"No, you won't do it."

"Yes, I will. One of us has to go in, and it's going to be me."

An armed member of the Fatah movement joins Palestinians in prayer before making a nationalistic speech to them in the village of Beit Our in Ramallah area.

"Do what you want, but don't tell anyone there where you spent the night."

"Coward," I joked.

"No, I'm just sane."

Morning came. I encouraged Majda to take part. She thought it would be a thrilling adventure, but apologized because she had to get back to Jerusalem. Our agent found someone to accompany me, despite the great irritation he displayed. My companion was a young local man, not a journalist, but a member of the PLO, which was better. We entered the old city through one of its main gates leading to the town market at Dawar Plaza in the center of the old city, a huge gate that never closes. Upon passing through the gate I found myself in a new world, the walls and floor of which were constructed of incredibly beautiful old stone. Its narrow passageways were just large enough to let a small tractor pass without running over the crowds of passersby. Commercial shops lined one next to another displayed their wares at their entrances. Customers found it difficult to stand inside the shops. Overhead, sheets of corrugated metal reached across the roofs of facing buildings to provide people and wares with shelter from the sun and rain. Daylight was diminished to the point I thought I was entering a city dug into the bowels of the earth.

From all sides arose the sounds of hawking vendors, haggling buyers, racing tractors, their drivers yelling to demand room to move, farmbirds squawking in poultry coops, and crying children being held tightly in arms. And there, too, came the sound of the call announcing it was time to perform the midday prayer.

Such were the markets in the old town of Nablus. The residential neighborhoods were no different than the markets, except that what had been shop doors were now doors to homes. Moving from one neighborhood to the next I passed through circular plazas that enabled the sun's rays to briefly carpet the ground as pedestrians split up to make room for others.

Everything was going along just fine. I saw no gallows or corpses. My companion talked to me about the town, its residents, and their respect for Black Panther members as the acting authority in the town. As we strolled, a group of men with covered faces appeared in front of us carrying Palestinian flags and marching through the alleyways. I remarked to my companion: "Those are not the Black Panthers, are they?"

"No, those are members of the Democratic Front, marching to assert their presence."

I started to take pictures, but he stopped me and indicated we would need to get permission from the masked men first. He went over and talked to one of them, and we got permission. I asked him to stay close by and not leave me alone, but he began clapping and jumping here and there to encourage them. I could still see him, but he was no longer nearby me.

The shouts of citizens rang throughout the area,

Palestinian demonstration in the West Bank Old City of Nablus.

announcing that Israeli army forces were about to storm the town and had reached the gates. Masked men, demonstrators, and citizens all ran off in different directions. I searched for my companion, but could not find him. He had also fled, and now I too had to get out of the area before the army patrols arrived and I would be detained on charges of engaging in news coverage inside a military area that had been officially declared closed to the news media.

I began running in the direction that most of the demonstrators had fled. I found myself going from neighborhood to neighborhood through passageways and alleys, not knowing where I was or what I had reached. I was lost and could no longer determine the direction from which I had come. I asked people how to get out of town, but no one would reply.

I kept on moving, escaping the intense stares and closed mouths, making my way through the crowd using my body and briefcase. Perplexed, I stopped at an intersection of alleys, not knowing whether to go right or left. Suddenly, the crowd dispersed except for a rectangular-faced young man standing directly in front of me, fixing me with a cold arrogant stare. Several other young men had surrounded me.

I examined the young man looking for any clue as to whom he might be. He was wearing a brown shirt and green military pants. On his hip hung a large black pistol, and a dagger was stuck inside the belt around his waist. What leapt into my mind was that he, and those surrounding me, might be an Israeli military squad that had penetrated the town to

*Commercial shops in Nablus have closed their doors after
clashes broke out between Palestinian demonstrators and Israeli forces.*

arrest demonstrators and had happened upon me. I quickly put the idea out of my mind, however, because townspeople had gathered around us, rather than running away in flight. So they must be who I thought they could be, and I hoped I was wrong.

The young man smiled arrogantly and asked: "What are you doing here?"

"I'm looking for a way out. I'm a Palestinian journalist from Jerusalem. I was covering the demonstration by the Democratic Front. Now I'm running away from the army and in need to get out of town."

"A journalist, wanting to get out of here? Ha!" he said derisively. He stepped close to me, then put my arms in the air and searched me, then my bag, perhaps looking for a weapon. His hands and clothes gave off an unusual and foul odor that I could not make out.

"Do you have any identification?" he asked, as he played with the top of my shirt, touching my throat with his fingertips.

I took out my wallet and showed him the *al-Fajr* newspaper card and my League of Arab Journalists I.D., giving him space to investigate before coming to a stupid decision. He grabbed the identity papers and wallet out of my hand and asked what they contained. I answered that he could find out for himself, since he was holding my wallet.

He asked those around me to bring me forward. Two young men grabbed my arms forcefully, one on each side, and pushed me to start walking. Then I was sure they were Black Panther members.

"What is this?" I said, objecting and refusing to walk.

"We want to have a quick chat with you."

"No, you're 'dragging' me, and everyone in town is going to think I'm a collaborator. I have no objection if you want me to follow you, but there's no need to strong-arm me."

I would not let fear control what I said and did. If he discovered I was frightened, he might think my fear was that of a captured enemy. So I showed confidence and willpower to make him think I was a Palestinian on his side, or even a member of his organization, one who had had a bad day and hated to be challenged. He opened his mouth again with that arrogant smile I so hated, and chided the two holding me: "I told you to bring him, not to drag him."

Thank God, they took their hands off me, and my heart beat a bit easier. The young man walked rapidly, and I walked rapidly behind him, all the while surrounded by the others. He began to run, and I ran with him and the rest. I looked at his weapon and started thinking about the questions they might ask and prepared answers to them. Where they were taking me did not matter; my only concern was that they believe me.

We proceeded past alleyways and houses, followed by the inhabitants' eyes. I prayed that none of them was an Israeli spy who might wrongly believe that I was related to the group. We moved beyond the residences and entered a section empty of life. When we reached some ruins that were once the front of a house, the armed young man asked everyone else to wait and ordered me to follow him inside.

He indicated that I should sit on a pile of rocks and sat down in front of me. I found myself in a room with the sky above it surrounded by old stone walls overgrown with weeds. Beneath my feet I was stepping on earth and tiles, and something else there that I could not determine. Upon entering the room, the first thing to attract my attention was the same unusual odor that had reached my nose earlier when I had met the man detaining me. In the room, however, the smell was even more intense and foul.

"Where are we?" I asked with interest.

"In the courtroom."

"Ah, the courtroom. I've heard a lot about it."

"From whom."

"From my companion, a local person I got separated from before running into you."

"Did he tell you about the drain?" he asked, pointing to a corner where there was something resembling the remains of a privy hole.

"I don't recall him speaking about a drain."

"The drain's where we slaughter a collaborator when we don't want to hang him."

I wished I could stop breathing the air around me, and were it not for an empty stomach, I would have vomited my soul out. He stood up and circled me. He was still going through my wallet papers as he began the investigation: For whom do I work? What am I doing here? Whom do I know? Who am I? Where do I live?

"But you don't speak like someone from Bethlehem," he said, suspecting the truthfulness of my reply.

"Yes, it's a Bethlehem accent!"

"Not true."

"I may have been affected by the accents of the various Palestinian regions I visit daily as a journalist, but I'm a resident of Bethlehem."

He believed me and moved on to a new point; however, I had learned a lesson from him, for I realized I should perfect the accent of Bethlehem's Muslims. Mine was Christian, and it was of no use to me when I got into a difficult situation in Muslim areas.

The investigation continued: "Do you want to photograph an execution?"

"I don't think so."

"Why not?"

"Because there's no way to guarantee the murder wasn't committed for the picture."

"The collaborator still has to be killed."

"You do your work, and God be with you, and I will take pictures of the corpses when I come across them."

"Do you want to photograph us?" He asked pointing his index finger at his chest, looking deeply into my eyes. I had hoped to photograph a Black Panther. It would be a media scoop and the dream of any photojournalist. But I sensed in his question a test, rather than a request.

"Of course not," I replied confidently.

"Why not?"

"To ensure your safety, and to avoid problems with Israeli intelligence."

He smiled and stopped asking questions. He looked at my camera and his face relaxed. He asked me if he could hold it, and I let him! He liked the camera and wanted to play with it. The way he held the camera indicated he had never had the chance to play with anything like it before. He asked about the various parts, which I explained to him.

With the question of a five-year-old, he asked me: "Can you take pictures from far away?" After I answered, he inquired at length about the nature of the work of a photojournalist.

He told me that he wanted to become one of us, but he was never able to accomplish any of that.

Four young men armed with rifles, pistols, and daggers hanging off their sides arrived at the "courtroom." The largest of them called the man detaining me by the name of Hani and asked for me. Hani introduced me to him and him to me as Alaa el-Din, the commander of the Black Panther group. He too asked some quick questions, but Hani's decision had been taken into consideration.

"How can you say your names in front of me, when you know that I'm a journalist?" I asked Alaa el-Din after engaging in a quick conversation with him and flattering his work and position.

"Because it's not important anymore. Israeli intelligence knows every one of us," he said simply.

A boy of no more than twelve entered. Panting and trying to catch his breath after a long run, he gave us the news: "The army . . . the army is on its way to here."

Alaa el-Din ordered the group to withdraw. Everyone got ready and then headed toward a hollow area atop the wall overlooking a dark alley. I stopped their leader, and Hani stopped with him:

"What about me?" I asked, objecting to being left by myself in the "courtroom" without the instructions I needed to get out of the town. Realizing his oversight, Alaa el-Din asked the panting boy to go with me.

The boy guided me through and over terrifying alleys in a different direction than that of the group. He ran swiftly and leapt like a monkey. My strength began to fail me. It was very hard to keep up with him because of the weight of the cameras and the cigarette smoke in my chest. Finally, the wall of the old city came into view in front of us, and then one of its exits, thank God.

The boy stopped a passing car and ordered the driver to take me wherever I wanted. Then he vanished in the distance, returning to the darkness of the town. The aged driver stared at me in fright and very politely asked where I was headed! "The Jerusalem taxi stand, if you would please," I responded.

I returned to Jerusalem and then to the newspaper office. I found Majda very nervously waiting for me to show up or to call. She had learned from our agent that I had gotten separated from my companion during the demonstration and that no one knew where I had gone. She asked me what had happened, and I told her.

I arrived home late that evening to find my mother had prepared a considerable dinner following my two-day absence. I ate without tasting and listened to everyone without speaking, and then went up to bed where I couldn't fall asleep. The long rectangular face, the black pistol, the drain, Alaa el-Din, and the boy simply hung there before my eyes; the smell of blood still suffocated me. Less than two weeks passed when we got the news that Israeli state security had eliminated the Black Panther cell. It had taken them by surprise, killing them in the barber shop where they hung out.

The newspapers published their pictures, among which were photos of Hani and Alaa el-Din. Not very long after that Israel also eliminated the Red Eagle cell.

75

An armed member of PLO patrols the village of Yatta in the Hebron area.

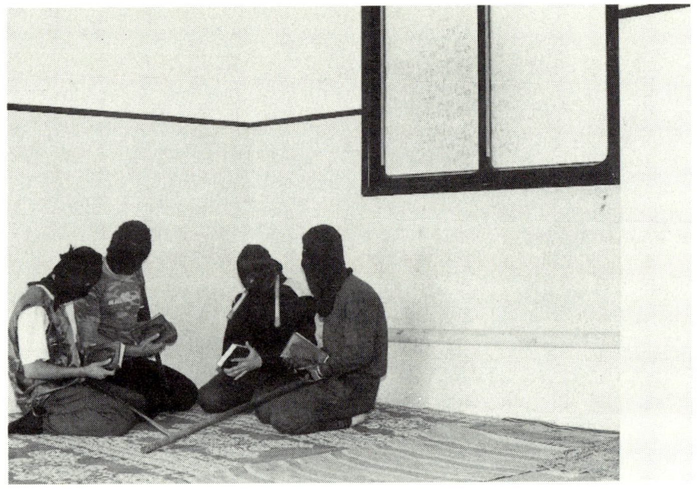

*A terrorist group from the Islamic Hamas movement meeting in a mosque
in Gaza City before carrying out "disciplinary" acts
against the town's citizens.*

People's Court

THE PALESTINIAN LEADERSHIP FOUGHT HARD against the Israeli presence to liberate the people and give them their rights, but it itself eliminated justice and upset peace. It did more to violate the rights of Palestinians than Israel did. It took away their freedom of choice and behavior and threatened their security and future.

The Islamic movements and the Palestinian Liberation Organization dispatched their members to all areas of East Jerusalem, the West Bank, and the Gaza Strip, using an iron fist to impose their authority, asserting that they were Palestinian strugglers and leadership representatives. They imposed their orders on the public and terrified everyone who refused to adhere to their policy.

Those leaders dragged the people into acts of violence

and crime. They sanctioned Palestinian murder of Jews, deeming such a crime to be a heroic act desired by God and man. The beating of Palestinian citizens and the shattering of their bones also became proper in order to "correct corruption" or to "discipline" society. If a citizen committed an error, the "strugglers" rushed to apply punishment, which was enforced using neither wisdom nor court. The Islamists and PLO members enjoyed their authoritative status and carried out punishment more to prove their existence and flex their muscles than for purposes of correction.

In the spring of 1990 I moved to work for the Associated Press news agency. The correspondent in Bethlehem contacted me to tell me that a "lunch" would take place at midday in al-Madbasa Square in the town. "Lunch" was the term we used to indicate that an event that deserved covering was likely to occur. Since our correspondent, Mousa al-Shaer, was himself a member of the PLO, we could depend on his reports. I hurried over to his office, not far from al-Madbasa Square, and it was not long before "lunch" took place. We rushed to the location to take pictures. A crowd of citizens had gathered to watch a number of youths wearing masks as they pulled a middle-aged Palestinian man out of his shop to "discipline" him. With their clubs and chains they set about beating him severely. After the beating they led him to an open area in front of the crowd. He could barely stand up. Nearby one of the masked youths was busy trying to get rid of a crying young woman, who stood there pleading for mercy for her brother and asking the crowd to help out.

The leader of the masked youths raised his hand to get his audience's attention. He read out the man's crime: addiction to drugs and the Fatah movement's certainty that he was also a dealer. Then came the punishment. All the blows that had rained down on his head and body was apparently not yet a punishment. The time for the true punishment was now at hand. The leader of the masked youths grabbed the man's shoulder with his left hand, and with his right hand he raised a thick club into an ostentatious position above his head ready to strike. Stupefied and exhausted, lacking all willpower, the victim stared at those assembled. With everyone watching, the club was driven into his leg with full force. The sound of shattering bones blocked out the sister's screaming, the spectators' gasps, and the cries of the children. No one deserved to witness that crushing of bone; not the assembled citizens, not the children who were there, not the sister, and not even the punished man himself. The sound I heard of bones splintering will never leave my memory, a deep strangled sound that causes one's heart to stop beating. The masked youths then fled. The young woman threw her body over her brother, who was writhing on the ground in pain. She cried out for help, but no one wanted or was brave enough to help. Many of those who had gathered turned their backs and moved away. Others continued to stand there, some enjoying the scene, others perhaps weeping silently.

I made my way back to Mousa's office, my mind a jumble, terrified by what I had seen. At the entrance to the building I found a place to sit down at the bottom of the stairs. I did not want to go up to the office or back out onto the street. I wondered what I could have done to prevent the incident from happening and keep the man's bones from being crushed. A horrid sense of guilt filled me because I had known something was going to happen, or more exactly, I knew someone would become a victim in that square at that time. Yet I had remained silent on the pretext that I am a journalist, or perhaps because I am a Palestinian.

As I sat at the entrance to the building, I was approached by Maha al-Sahouria on her way to Mousa's office, where her sister worked as a secretary. Maha was a young Palestinian woman active politically in the Democratic Front. She came up to me and asked, "Why are you sitting here, Issam?"

"I need to take a break from the world," I answered quietly.

Sitting down beside me, she started to converse: "I saw you taking pictures of the beating in the square."

I didn't respond.

"The sound of the bones shattering was so violent," she added, and I remained silent.

"I could not believe what I was seeing. What happened went beyond all limits," she stressed. I still would not say a word.

"Something is wrong . . . There's something wrong . . . This cannot be right . . . ," she said, overcome. And in the silence, tears fell from our eyes.

Also in East Jerusalem, in the summer of 1992, dozens of young "strugglers" raced over to the tourist garden known as the Sultans' Tombs to watch the disciplining of a young man and woman after they had done what was considered corruption. The two were strolling in the garden after school let out and had been kissing each other. They were seen by a member of the PLO, who had been following them, perhaps out of jealousy. He notified his commander, who had come quickly to "discipline" them.

I was meeting with a number of journalists at the office of the al-Hakawati Theater, adjacent to the garden. Upon hearing the news, my colleagues (Mohammed al-Zahaikeh and Khalid al-Saeu) and I hurried over to the place. The young man had already been the recipient of ruthless punches and blows and had been let go. Now it was the girl's turn. She stood in her school uniform in the middle of the garden area. Her "discipliner" stood in the center of a wide circle surrounded by the "strugglers."

"Open your bag! I want to inspect it," the commander began contemptuously.

"Who are you to inspect it?" the 17 or 18-year-old girl asked.

"Open it or else."

"Or else what?"

He responded with a slap that sent her flying and filled her face with the redness of blood. He grabbed the bag violently, opened it, and pawed through its contents. The young woman straightened up confidently, holding her head high and showing her determination. With delicate fingertips she brushed locks of dark hair back from her soft petite face.

Full of himself and having found an excuse in the bag for continuing his rebuke, the commander turned to the young woman, "Why would a student need to take makeup with her to school?"

"You have no business asking that."

He slapped her once more, making her face even redder, and now blue, and again began digging through her bag. A surprise was awaiting him: a folded Palestinian flag carefully concealed so Israeli security officers would not find it were they also to search her. I really believed that the flag would earn that young woman a bit of mercy. Its presence in her possession indicated that she was certainly a struggler for Palestine, but unfortunately our commander grew even more contemptuous of her.

"A whore carrying the Palestinian flag. Palestine doesn't need the likes of you!"

"I'm more honorable than you are," she replied with confidence and courage deserving applause. He slapped her for the third time with all his might. He lifted his arm in the air and hit her across her face near the ear. She staggered and fell to the ground. She stood back up, struggling with herself to keep from crying. He recorded her name from the cover of one of her notebooks and stuffed the flag in his pocket. Then, cocky and disdainful, he threw her bag and the rest of her things at her, ending what he did not consider to have been disciplining her.

"This time I'll let you go, but we are going to keep track of you. If you do anything immoral again, we will discipline you and inform your parents about it. Now, pick up your things and get out of here."

The young woman crept around the ground gathering her things, which were scattered amidst the feet of the "strugglers." My colleagues and I were observing from near the gate to the garden. We looked at each other, totally ashamed of what we had seen. We could not take any pictures and had agreed not to report the news for the sake of the young woman. Palestinian media institutions would distort the report to serve PLO interests, and were we to provide it to the Israeli or international media, we would face problems with the Palestinians.

Everyone began walking out of the garden, with the young woman at the rear. Outside the iron gate, which the garden guard had closed at the request of the strugglers, a large number of citizens and students had gathered to witness the event. The news had spread through the area. The "strugglers," of course, always made sure they brought their actions to everyone's attention to demonstrate their presence.

Near the gate, the guard's room was open, with his wife sitting inside. He had stayed at the gate to open it for those leaving and to prevent anyone on the outside from getting in. The young woman passed in front of me on her way to the gate. I called out to her: "I don't think you want to leave the garden right now. It might be better to wait in the guard's room with his wife until the crowds break up outside." I addressed her in a somewhat haughty manner to avoid bringing any problems with the "strugglers" down on myself, but I gave her a look of respect which she understood to mean I was seeking her best interest. She headed toward the guard at the gate, looking hopefully at him. The guard stood in front of her, blocking her path to his room. He had heard my proposal and understood the plea in her eyes. Instead he opened the garden gate for her, and as the clamor of the crowds intensified outside, he announced to her that he was an honorable man and does not receive whores in his room.

The young woman passed through the gate without hesitation. She covered her face with both hands, and with her shoulders forced a path through the crowd. She began to cry; she began to sob. She had finally succumbed to her ordeal. The tears fell, and her blood boiled. She quickly moved away until she disappeared from sight. Some distance away, a few "strugglers" followed her.

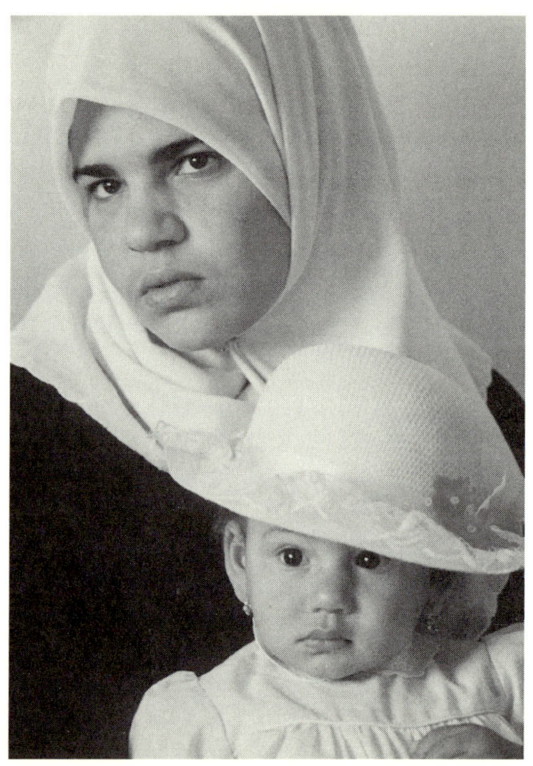

Mother and child.

Eyes of an Innocent to Eyes of a Terrorist

~

I WAS 14 YEARS OLD WHEN FOR THE FIRST TIME I found myself living as a Palestinian under Israeli occupation. It had been a week since my family and I had returned from Saudi Arabia to live in Bethlehem. It was late one cold winter night, and I was in the company of Yousef al-Natsheh, a Muslim young man whom I had recently gotten to know. We walked hurriedly down al-Madbasa Road toward the town market and its church and mosque. The wind had grown stronger when I turned to look back. I gasped and froze where I was. Yousef whispered to me nervously:

"Don't be afraid. Just keep walking and act naturally."

"I'm not afraid."

"Yes, you are," he scolded. "Just keep walking."

I was not so much frightened as I was surprised by the appearance of a military patrol out of the depths of darkness just a few steps away from me. The immense Jeep looked like a tank. The Israeli soldiers in the back of the Jeep, clasping their machine guns, were wrapped up in military overcoats against the rainy night. Neither of us said anything as the patrol rolled slowly by us. The eyes of the soldiers were like nails in us, hard and steely. I felt like prey, and they were the hunters. Then, for a few brief moments they looked to me like apprehensive eyes surveying their menacer. It left me wondering who was the menace, and who the victim.

Lengthy and exhausting days and years passed living in Bethlehem as a Palestinian cowering under the Israeli occupation, as a Christian capitulated to Islamic oppression, and as a journalist working in an atmosphere of political intolerance and absolutism. My work as a journalist led me to realize the fact that all of us, Palestinians and Israelis, have made ourselves the victims of our actions, and that it is essential that we work seriously to find a way to live together in peace, respecting the rights of all regarding freedom of choice and behavior in the context of common national and social obligations.

As a journalist I was a spokesman for the people, not politics. I expressed my opinion on the pressing need to give the Palestinian public free and honest news media and to

One generation leaves, another comes, and the conflict continues.

Christian theatrical group was directed by the author in Bethlehem.

acknowledge their right to choose and express their opinions without control or political distortion. Unfortunately, my work threatened my security, my ideas encountered the harsh censure of the PLO and the Islamic movements, and I found myself compelled to emigrate from my country to escape threat and flee oppression.

When the spring of 1993 approached, I had the opportunity to emigrate to the United States of America. I had the opportunity to flee, as did others, but many could not, and to this day cannot, escape.

In leaving my country, I left behind my family, my work, and everything and everyone I loved. I left my heart there too, to bleed in grief on its soil. Ten years have now passed since I emigrated, and yet there is no improvement in that region's conditions. Instead of improving, the dispute has intensified and violence is at its peak. The peace talks have been useless, and the peoples of the Holy Land have been drawn into a life filled with more horrible tragedies and deeper pain. Battlefields have become sown fields of war. Stones are little used anymore; the Palestinian people are now armed and Israel has exchanged its small arms for heavy weapons. Extremist Islamists have declared the *jihad* against the world, as well as against Israel, and murder and destruction have spread everywhere. Because of our cause the world bleeds blood, tears, and pain. The terror of our dispute has reached the homes of the innocent and ripped thousands apart.

Peoples and governments are seeking a solution for the

conflict, and yet there can be no solution unless people's rights are placed above the name of religion or ethnicity, the interests of the citizen are allowed to override political titles, and the disputing parties adopt unification and understanding as their means rather than differentiation and division.

This continuing dispute of ours is not worthy of a tear from a child's eye. It is our duty to work immediately to protect our children and ourselves from our dispute and to try to establish true peace and justice, if not for ourselves, then for our children and the future generations of the world. I left my country to flee from threat and leave terrorism behind, but terrorism has followed me to my new home, hurling its wrath on innocents who have no relation to our conflict and our causes. These innocent people received us in their homes with wide-open arms, not knowing our language or being able to pronounce our names correctly. In exchange, we have presented them with scenes of crime and terror uglier and more perverse than even those we gave ourselves.

Here in my new homeland, confronted with terrorism, I again began to write. I wrote about the past in which I had lived, and in which I had laughed and cried. I found my self responsible to share with the public what I know about the general way of thinking and behavior of the Muslims of the Middle East, and to introduce the basic sources from which Islamic terrorism springs. Perhaps by learning of its origins we will be able to fight it at its roots and provide our country and communities with permanent peace and security.

By writing this book and the series of my complete works, I know that I have sentenced myself to an obscure future of pursuit and difficulties. Nonetheless, I am certain that I will find happiness, and perhaps I can help make others happy. By writing, I will free myself from the captivity of the past and attempt to accomplish a task that brings due meaning to my suffering and that of my family, the people of my homeland and new country, and those I love. Perhaps by writing, I also will be able to rid myself of those looks that continue to haunt me night and day; looks of a child that do not allow me to forget them, looks that ask questions for which I have no answer. I met that child during a press coverage tour I made with Essais in the Gaza Strip.

"Stop," I asked the driver from Gaza who was taking us around the sandy streets of the al-Shati refugee camp in his old Peugeot. Essais and I had left our cars at the Erez crossing outside the city and had hired a local car and driver. Driving our cars with Israeli license plates inside the Strip was equivalent to suicide. The Strip had its own plates, and any car bearing an Israeli license would be demolished and its occupants attacked.

"Stop," I repeated. "Wait here; I'll be right back."

"What are you doing?" Essais asked nervously as he jumped out of the back seat to follow me.

"I'm going to take a picture."

"What picture?"

A Palestinian child carrying a sign on which is written "Peace" in Arabic, Hebrew, and English during a demonstration in Bethlehem.

"The picture of a child, that child."

"You've gotten out of the car in the middle of the camp carrying cameras, arousing suspicion about all of us, and threatening our safety to take a child's picture?"

"Yes, to take a child's picture."

"What's so important about the child's picture?"

"The child."

"What's so important about the child?"

"The child! Look, he's wearing the turban of a Muslim sheikh. Look at him. He's just a kid, no more than five years old, but his head is weighted down with a turban and an Islamic robe constricts his movement. Look at him. He's carrying an ice cream cone in his hand. He certainly doesn't need that turban on his head or heavy clothing in this heat. He needs freedom. Surely he wants to play. How will he be able to play wearing that robe? Look at the robe. It's not clothing for a special occasion, it's for everyday. Someone dressed him up in it and that turban . . . his father or mother, or perhaps a sheikh. It is impossible for a child of his age to wrap a turban that well. One of them did it and perhaps told him that God, Most High, wanted him to do that so he would not say no."

I approached him and began taking pictures. My eye fastened on his eye through the lens. I did not know whether he thought I was proud of him, like the others around him, for having obeyed the will of God, Most High, or whether he was viewing me as a savior who would tear his burden off his head and rip apart his robe. I could not know. I took the pictures as he silently watched me with his wide eyes. His face looked like the face of any child in my Christian neighborhood or on an Israeli street. He looked like any child, whether was a Muslim, a Christian, or a Jew.

I drew in a breath, and my fingers stopped taking pictures. For a moment I saw in the child's eyes my own eyes when I was his age. I saw in him me when I was a child. I put the camera back on my shoulder; Essais was also taking pictures. I moved away, pulling back from my view of the child. I hurried away so I could resist taking him with me far away from the Strip. I wanted to take him with me to protect him from the future to which he was destined, and to prevent his eyes . . . his innocent eyes . . . from one day, some day, becoming those of a terrorist.

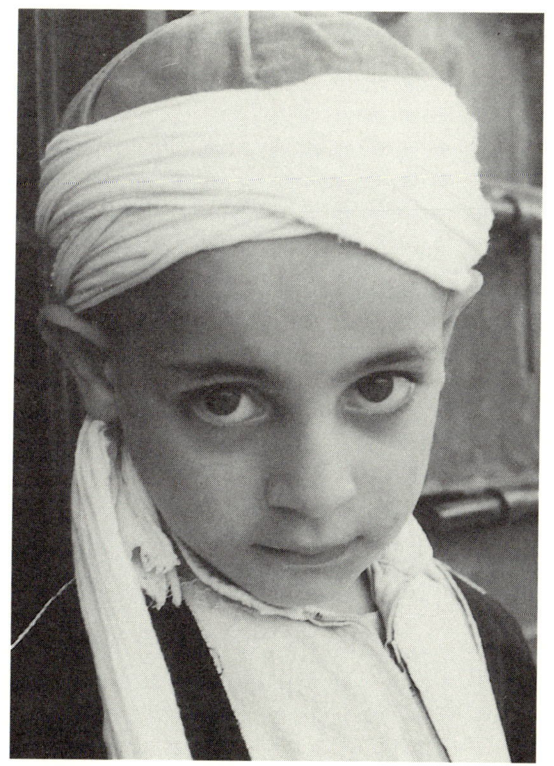

The child in Gaza.